D0793349

CROSS-SECTIONS
THE M270 MULTIPLE
ROCKET LAUNCHER

by Steve Parker
illustrated by Alex Pang

Capstone press

Mankato, Minnesota

Edge Books are published by Capstone Press, a Coughlan Publishing Company.
151 Good Counsel Drive, P.O. Box 669, Mankato, Minnesota 56002.
www.capstonepress.com

Library of Congress Cataloging-in-Publication Data
Parker, Steve.
    The M270 multiple rocket launcher/by Steve Parker; illustrated by Alex Pang.
    p. cm.—(Edge books. Cross-sections.)
    Summary: "An in-depth look at the M270 Multiple Rocket Launcher, with
detailed cross-section diagrams, action photos, and fascinating facts"—Provided
by publisher.
    Includes bibliographical references and index.
    ISBN-13: 978-1-4296-0096-5 (hardcover)
    ISBN-10: 1-4296-0096-9 (hardcover)
    1. Rocket launchers (Ordnance)—Juvenile literature. I. Title.
UF880.P37 2008
623.4'2—dc22   2007010619

Designed and produced by

David West ☊☊ Children's Books
7 Princeton Court
55 Felsham Road
Purney
London SW15 1AZ

Designer: Gary Jeffrey
Editor: Gail Bushnell

Photo Credits
Frank Ontiveros, 1, 4–5, 25; wikipedia.org, 6, 7t; DoD photo, 11, 22; SPC TEDDY
WADE; USA, 13; SSGT Kalmanson, 15; U.S. Army, 24, 28–29; U.S. Army photo by
Spc. Alisan Gul, 17; Ted Gaskins, 18, 19; DoD photo by Staff Sgt. Jim Varhegyi, U.S.
Air Force, 20; Spc. Russell J. Good, 28l; National Air Intelligence Center, 7b

1 2 3 4 5 6 12 11 10 09 08 07

TABLE OF CONTENTS

The M270 MLRS 4

Rocket Launcher History. 6

Cross-Section 8

Wheels and Tracks. 10

Engine 12

The Launcher 14

M26 Rocket 16

MGM-140 Missile 18

M270 Crew 20

Driver's Station 22

M270 Systems 24

The Mission 26

The Future 28

Glossary 30

Read More 31

Internet Sites. 31

Index 32

THE M270 MLRS

The M270 Multiple Launch Rocket System
(MLRS) is a mobile launcher for surface-to-surface
rockets and various missiles. The M270 is based
on an armored vehicle with tracks like a tank.
The vehicle carries a launcher that holds
two pods, each containing six rockets or
one larger missile.

The M270 MLRS uses its firepower against enemy vehicles, buildings, and bases. It can also take out enemy surface-to-air weapons to prepare the way for aircraft and missile strikes.

ROCKET LAUNCHER HISTORY

The Soviet (Russian) Katyusha BM-13 had a row of rails fixed onto a ZiS-6 truck. The 16 M-13 rockets slid along the rails as they took off.

The first rocket launchers were made more than 400 years ago in Korea. They used gunpowder to fire up to 200 exploding arrows from a handcart!

KATYUSHAS

In World War II (1939–1945), the Soviet army first used its Katyusha BM series of multiple rocket launchers. These launchers fired many rockets, one after the other, from the back of trucks.

SCREAMING MIMI

Another World War II launcher was the six-tube Nebelwerfer. It was called "Screaming Mimi" from the noise of its rocket blast-offs.

The German Nebelwerfer was not self-propelled. This means it had no engine, so it had to be towed.

MASS DESTRUCTION

Early rocket launchers were slow and difficult to aim. But if the rockets reached their target, they rained down huge destruction on the enemy. Over the

In the 1960s, the Russian BM-21 was used by more countries than any other launcher.

years, the U.S. military has altered various armored vehicles to become rocket launchers. These launchers aim rockets more accurately than early launchers did, and they also launch guided missiles.

In the Gulf War (1991), Iraq used Scud missile launchers. Scud missiles were developed in the 1950s. They are powerful but somewhat inaccurate.

CROSS-SECTION

The M270's various parts, including the vehicle, launcher, and rockets, all work together as one weapons system.

More than 800 M270s have been built for the U.S. military. Other countries have helped design, improve, and build the M270, including the United Kingdom, France, Germany, and Italy. Another 10 countries have bought M270s for their armies.

M26 ROCKET
See pages 16–17

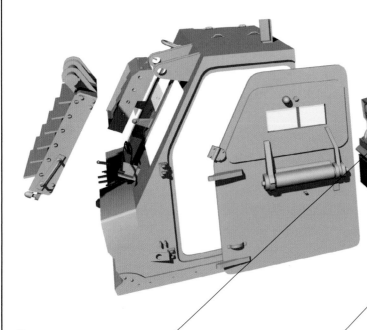

CREW COMPARTMENT
See pages 20–21

DRIVER'S STATION
See pages 22–23

ENGINE
See pages 12–13

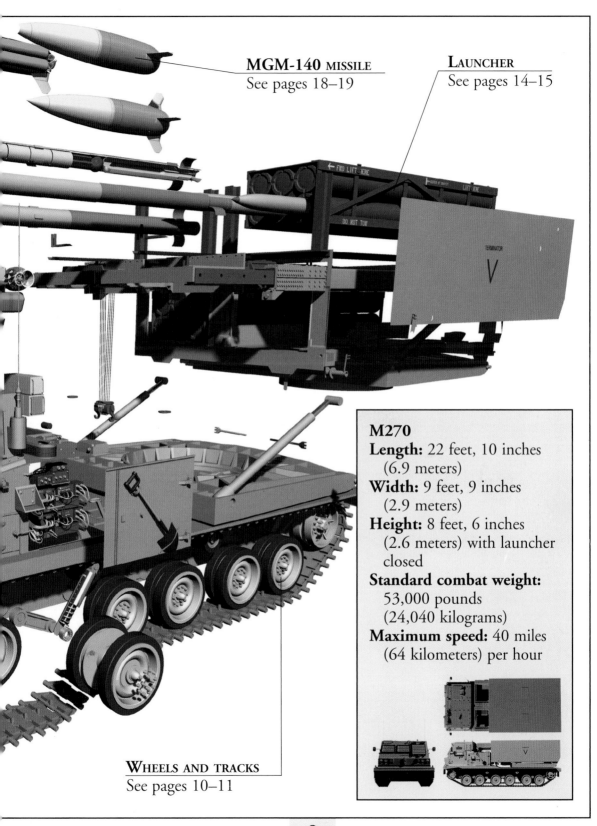

MGM-140 MISSILE
See pages 18–19

LAUNCHER
See pages 14–15

M270
Length: 22 feet, 10 inches
(6.9 meters)
Width: 9 feet, 9 inches
(2.9 meters)
Height: 8 feet, 6 inches
(2.6 meters) with launcher
closed
Standard combat weight:
53,000 pounds
(24,040 kilograms)
Maximum speed: 40 miles
(64 kilometers) per hour

WHEELS AND TRACKS
See pages 10–11

WHEELS AND TRACKS

The main parts of the M270 are based on the M2 Bradley infantry fighting vehicle. The M2 Bradley is the main U.S. battlefield troop carrier. The M270's engine, wheels, tracks, and frame, or chassis, all come from the Bradley.

The Bradley's chassis has been lengthened, or stretched, to carry the M270 launcher. Tracks allow the vehicle to climb steep slopes and even cross soft mud without getting stuck.

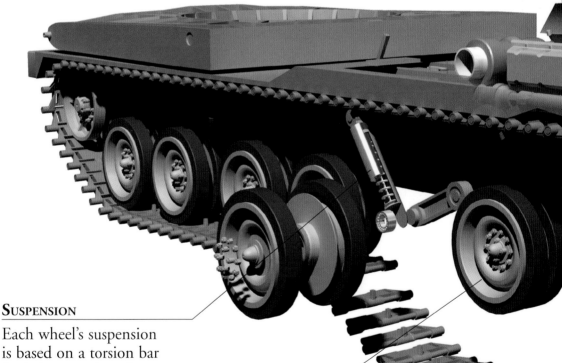

SUSPENSION

Each wheel's suspension is based on a torsion bar (twisting metal arm). The two front and two rear road wheels have shock absorbers, known as hydraulic dampers.

ROAD WHEELS

The six road wheels are in three groups of two. Their rubber tires give a fairly smooth ride as the track passes beneath.

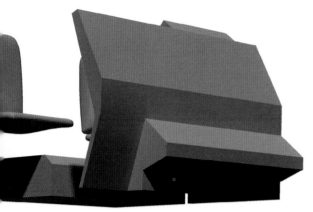

The M270 speeds along ordinary roads. It can cross a trench 8 feet (2.4 meters) wide and climbs over objects up to 2 feet, 6 inches (0.7 meters) high.

DRIVE WHEELS

The two drive wheels (one on each side) are the only two powered by the engine. Each drive wheel has 11 rod-like teeth that fit into the gaps in the track. The teeth make the track loop around and around like a "rolling road."

TRACK

On each side, the total length of track in contact with the ground is 14 feet, 2 inches (4.3 meters). The left track has 89 links, or shoes. The right track has 88. Each shoe has a replaceable rubber pad.

ENGINE

The M270 is powered by a huge turbo diesel engine, as used in the M2 Bradley. It is positioned behind and under the crew cabin.

The diesel engine can run on ordinary diesel fuel. It can also use JP-8, which is a type of jet fuel used by many military planes and vehicles. With full tanks, the M270 can cover about 300 miles (480 kilometers).

STEERING UNIT

If the driver steers very sharply, one track moves while the other one stays still. This makes the M270 almost spin around on the spot.

Control column

Position of engine on the M270

TRANSMISSION AND FINAL DRIVE

The HMPT 500-3EC gearbox is automatic. It chooses one of three gears. It assesses the vehicle's weight. It also checks if it is going up or down a slope.

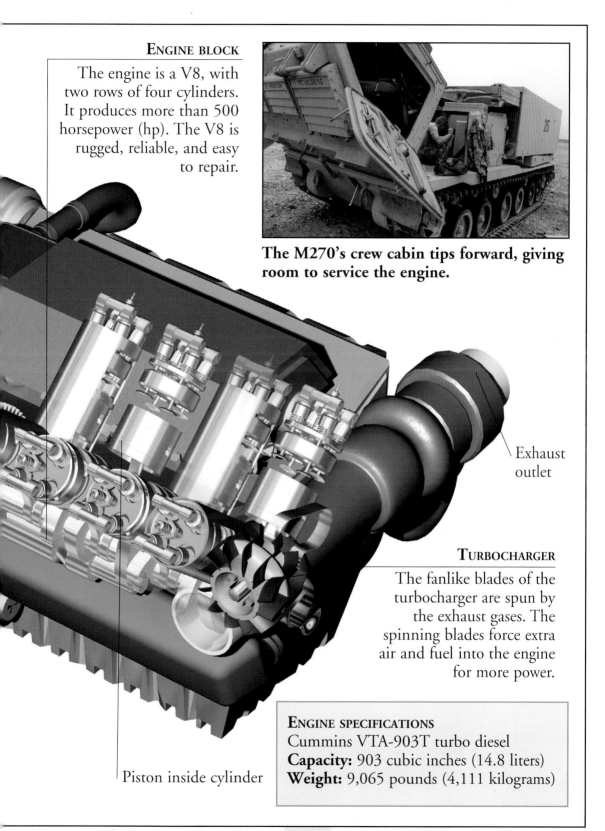

ENGINE BLOCK

The engine is a V8, with two rows of four cylinders. It produces more than 500 horsepower (hp). The V8 is rugged, reliable, and easy to repair.

The M270's crew cabin tips forward, giving room to service the engine.

Exhaust outlet

TURBOCHARGER

The fanlike blades of the turbocharger are spun by the exhaust gases. The spinning blades force extra air and fuel into the engine for more power.

Piston inside cylinder

ENGINE SPECIFICATIONS
Cummins VTA-903T turbo diesel
Capacity: 903 cubic inches (14.8 liters)
Weight: 9,065 pounds (4,111 kilograms)

The Launcher

The M270 is also called an SPLL, or Self-Propelled Launch-Loader. In an emergency, one person can load the rockets, drive the M270 into position, and aim and fire the rockets.

The Bradley-based vehicle that carries the launcher is code named the M993. The launcher itself is the M269. The launcher has powerful electric motors to turn or swivel on its turret. It turns in a full circle in just a few seconds.

The weapons pods slide into the launcher using the M270's boom and hoist like a built-in crane.

Hydraulic arm

TERMINATOR

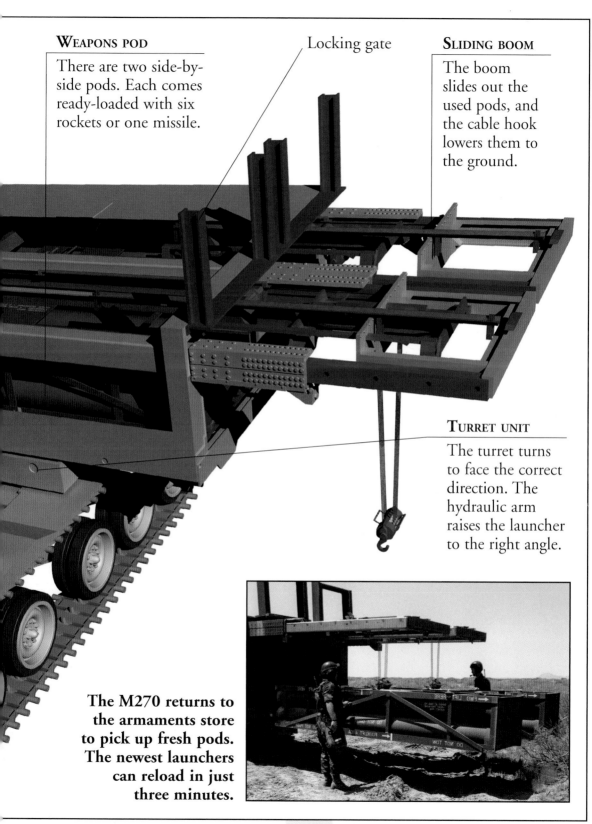

WEAPONS POD

There are two side-by-side pods. Each comes ready-loaded with six rockets or one missile.

Locking gate

SLIDING BOOM

The boom slides out the used pods, and the cable hook lowers them to the ground.

TURRET UNIT

The turret turns to face the correct direction. The hydraulic arm raises the launcher to the right angle.

The M270 returns to the armaments store to pick up fresh pods. The newest launchers can reload in just three minutes.

M26 ROCKET

The basic rocket fired by the M270 is called the M26. It has been improved over the years to go farther and carry more destructive power.

Fuse

Drag ribbon

Explosive charge

Steel frag case

The basic M26 rocket can travel more than 20 miles (32 kilometers). Later versions have a larger motor and can go more than twice as far.

Each M77 bomblet charge explodes its steel casing as it hits the ground. The casing shatters into more than 100 pieces that blast apart over a wide area.

FUSE

The fuse is timed by electronics to set off an explosive charge in the middle of the rocket. This blows the rocket apart in midair, releasing the bomblets.

BASIC M26 ROCKET
Length: 13 feet (3.9 meters)
Width: 9 inches (22.8 centimeters)
Weight: approximately 660 pounds (300 kilograms) depending on payload

M77 BOMBLETS

The main payload compartment is packed with explosives, in this case 644 M77 bomblets. These scatter and explode on impact.

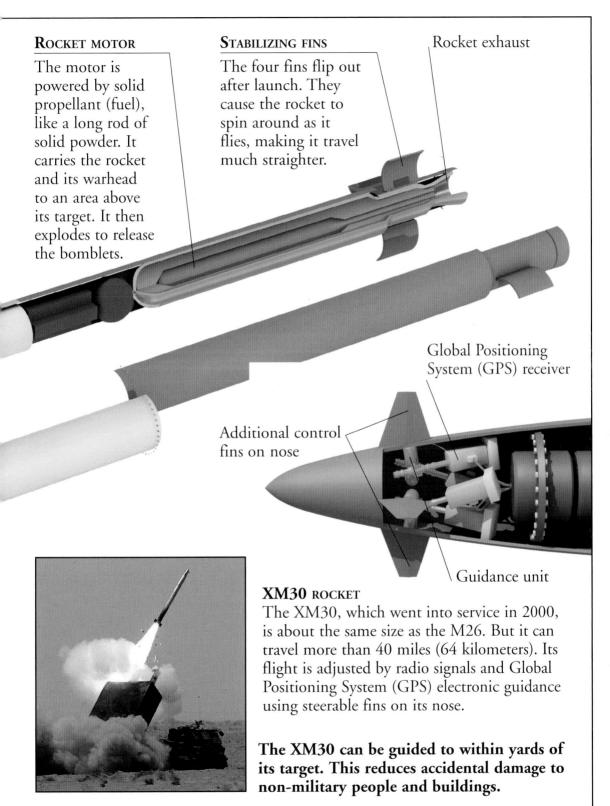

ROCKET MOTOR

The motor is powered by solid propellant (fuel), like a long rod of solid powder. It carries the rocket and its warhead to an area above its target. It then explodes to release the bomblets.

STABILIZING FINS

The four fins flip out after launch. They cause the rocket to spin around as it flies, making it travel much straighter.

Rocket exhaust

Global Positioning System (GPS) receiver

Additional control fins on nose

Guidance unit

XM30 ROCKET

The XM30, which went into service in 2000, is about the same size as the M26. But it can travel more than 40 miles (64 kilometers). Its flight is adjusted by radio signals and Global Positioning System (GPS) electronic guidance using steerable fins on its nose.

The XM30 can be guided to within yards of its target. This reduces accidental damage to non-military people and buildings.

MGM-140 MISSILE

The U.S. MGM-140 is known as the ATACMS, or Army Tactical Missile System. The MGM-140 can release a rain of cluster bomblets or carry one single high-penetration explosive.

Development of the MGM-140 began in 1982 and its first tests were in 1988. An improved version with longer range, the MGM-140B, went into service in 1998.

All is quiet when suddenly the MGM-140 roars into the sky and speeds to its target.

GUIDANCE SECTION

The nose cone contains the electronic circuits and GPS equipment. This guidance system tells the missile exactly where it is as it flies.

M74 bomblet

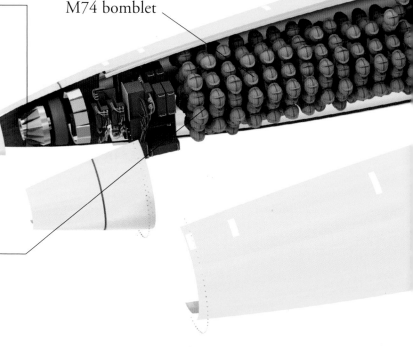

PAYLOAD SECTION

The MGM-140B has 275 M74 bomblets in its payload compartment.

M74 BOMBLETS
Each ball-shaped bomblet is about the size of a small apple. Hundreds fall to the ground like deadly exploding hailstones.

The MGM-140 is powered by a rocket engine. The missile can reach a target 180 miles (289 kilometers) away in less than five minutes.

Fuse

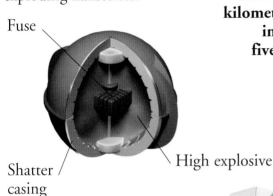

Shatter casing

High explosive

CONTROL SECTION
The control fins |adjust to steer the missile toward its target.

ROCKET MOTOR SECTION
The large solid fuel rocket allows the MGM-140B to travel more than 180 miles (289 kilometers).

MGM-140 MISSILE
Length: 13 feet (3.9 meters)
Width: 2 feet (0.6 meters)
Weight: 2,910 pounds (1,319 kilograms)

M270 CREW

The M270 has a crew of three: commander, driver, and gunner. Each one learns about the others' jobs and can take over the M270 in an emergency.

The commander has on-the-spot control. He decides where to go, what to attack, and when to fire. He uses the radio to stay in touch with other vehicles. The main base at central command sends advice and orders by radio too.

COMMANDER

The commander sits or stands on the right of the crew cabin. He scans the scene for signs of the enemy. He talks on the radio to central command as they discuss and decide tactics.

This commander is talking on the intercom to his driver as they approach a firing site.

GUNNER

The gunner's screen displays the direction and distance (range) of targets. He makes sure the rockets or missiles are armed and ready to fire.

DRIVER

The driver steers carefully around obstacles. He watches for dangers, such as disturbed earth that could cover land mines.

DRIVER'S STATION

The driver controls the M270 much like an ordinary automobile. But the M270 is 15 times heavier. The M270 can also climb steep slopes that most vehicles would slide back down.

The accelerator pedal controls the engine speed, and the brake pedal slows the M270. The auto transmission lever selects from a range of speeds for the three gears. The U-shaped steering yoke works in the same way as a typical steering wheel.

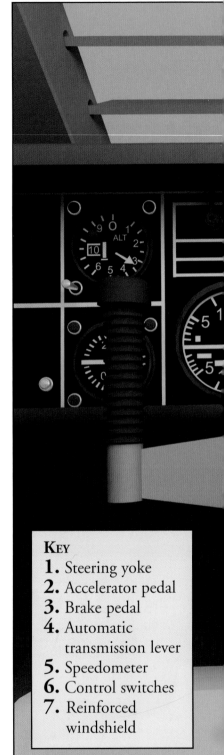

The front window is made from specially strengthened glass. The blast shutters help stop explosions from shattering it.

KEY
1. Steering yoke
2. Accelerator pedal
3. Brake pedal
4. Automatic transmission lever
5. Speedometer
6. Control switches
7. Reinforced windshield

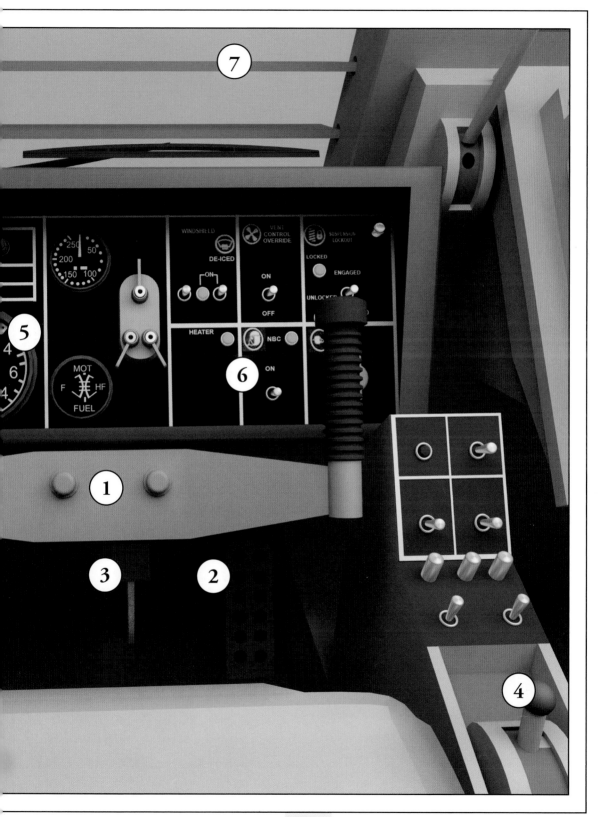

M270 SYSTEMS

The M270 has many systems for different jobs. Several have back-ups in case the main system fails or suffers damage from enemy fire.

The fire control panel is in the crew cabin. It is linked by wires to the fire control unit in the launcher. This sets off the rockets or missiles. The stabilizer checks the tilt or angle of the vehicle and the launcher's aim. The computer adjusts the aim after a rocket or missile fires in case the tilt has changed.

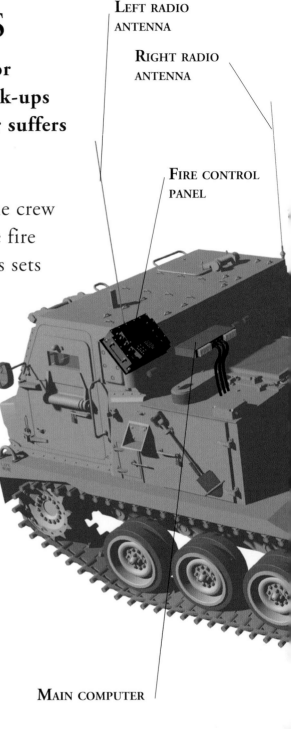

LEFT RADIO ANTENNA

RIGHT RADIO ANTENNA

FIRE CONTROL PANEL

MAIN COMPUTER

The Fire Control System (FCS) can be operated by the M270's gunner (above) or receive target information from central command by radio.

The M270 can fire its rockets one by one. It can also launch all 12 within a minute, one after the other, in a ripple firing.

MAIN ELECTRONIC UNIT

RELOAD BOOM CONTROLLER

FIRE CONTROL UNIT

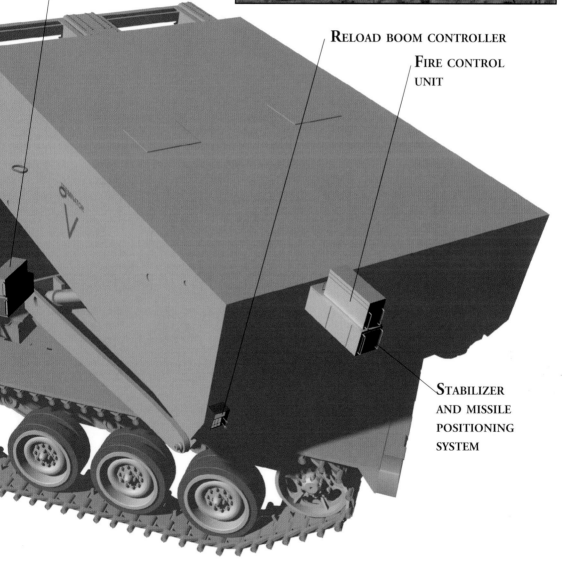

STABILIZER AND MISSILE POSITIONING SYSTEM

THE MISSION

The great range of the M270's rockets and missiles means it can usually stay well behind the battlefront.

1. Two M270s take up support positions behind the combat front line. They wait to receive instructions from central command.

The smoke and heat from the M270's weapons are easily detected by the enemy. The M270 uses stealth to get into position and then fires its rockets or missiles. After firing, it moves away before its position is pinpointed. This tactic is called "shoot and scoot."

④

5. Meanwhile the two M270s speed away to avoid becoming targets themselves.

6. At another location the second M270 launches one guided missile. It is aimed at an enemy bunker. The bunker is destroyed. The MLRSs head home to reload.

4. Thirty miles (48 kilometers) away, the rockets hit the target—a forward command post. It is totally destroyed.

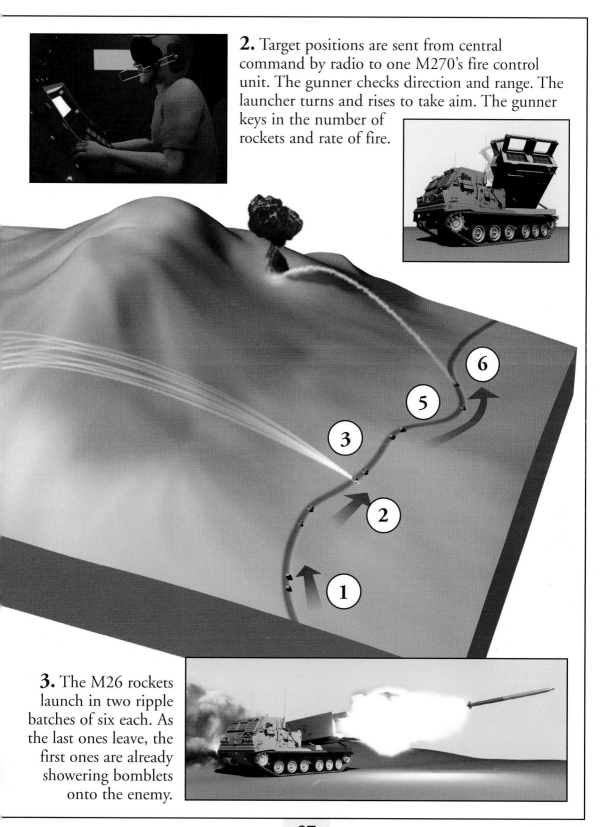

2. Target positions are sent from central command by radio to one M270's fire control unit. The gunner checks direction and range. The launcher turns and rises to take aim. The gunner keys in the number of rockets and rate of fire.

3. The M26 rockets launch in two ripple batches of six each. As the last ones leave, the first ones are already showering bomblets onto the enemy.

THE FUTURE

The first M270s went into service in 1982. They have seen action in several wars, with great success. They have fired more than 10,000 rockets.

The year 2000 saw the first improved M270A1s in action. Their fire control system is more accurate and the launcher turns and tilts faster. There are plans to build more than 1,600 M270s and up to 480,000 M26-type rockets. This will take until well past 2015.

A newer multiple rocket launcher is the "six-pack" High Mobility Artillery Rocket System (HIMARS). It may take over some roles from the M270 in the coming years.

The High Mobility Artillery Rocket System fires the same rockets as the M270. It is smaller, faster, and has tires, not tracks.

The M270A1 has many improved features over the M270. It can reload faster, aim quicker, and shoot more accurately. The M270 family of rockets and missiles is also constantly upgraded.

GLOSSARY

armor (AR-mur)—a protective metal covering

chassis (CHASS-ee)—the main framework of a vehicle to which the other parts are fixed

exhaust (eg-ZAWST)—very hot gases leaving an engine

horsepower (HORSS-pou-ur)—the measurement of an engine's power, abbreviated as hp

payload (pay-LOWD)—something carried by a vehicle, rocket, or missile, which in warfare is often a warhead or explosives

suspension (suss-PEN-shun)—the tilting arms, springs, dampers, and other parts that smooth out road bumps so a vehicle's ride is more comfortable

track (TRAK)—on a tank or tracked vehicle, the links that form an endless loop, like a conveyor belt or "rolling road"

transmission (tranz-MISH-uhn)—gears and other parts that transfer the power from the engine to the wheels

READ MORE

Baker, David. *M2A2 Bradley Fighting Vehicle.* Fighting Forces. Vero Beach, Fla.: Rourke, 2007.

Dartford, Mark. *Missiles and Rockets.* Military Hardware in Action. Minneapolis: Lerner, 2003.

Graham, Ian. *Military Vehicles.* Designed for Success. Chicago: Heinemann, 2003.

INTERNET SITES

FactHound offers a safe, fun way to find Internet sites related to this book. All of the sites on FactHound have been researched by our staff.

Here's how:
1. Visit *www.facthound.com*
2. Choose your grade level.
3. Type in this book ID **1429600969** for age-appropriate sites. You may also browse subjects by clicking on letters, or by clicking on pictures and words.
4. Click on the **Fetch It** button.

FactHound will fetch the best sites for you!

INDEX

ATACMS (Army Tactical Missile System). *See* MGM-140 missile

bomblets, 16–17, 18, 19, 27
  M74 bomblets, 18–19
  M77 bomblets, 16

chassis, 10
commander, 20

driver, 12, 20, 21, 22

engine, 6, 10, 11, 12–13, 19, 22

fire control system, 24, 28
fuel, 12
fuse, 16, 19

Global Positioning System (GPS), 17, 18
gunner, 20, 21, 24, 27

High Mobility Artillery Rocket System (HIMARS), 28

Katyusha BM series launchers, 6, 7

M2 Bradley, 10, 12
M26 rocket, 8, 16–17, 27, 28
M269 launcher section, 8, 14–15
M993 vehicle, 14
MGM-140 missile, 18–19

Nebelwerfer, 6

ripple firing, 25, 27

Scud missiles, 7
"shoot and scoot", 26–27
steering, 12, 21, 22

tracks, 4, 10–11, 12, 28
transmission, 12, 22
turbocharger, 13

weapons pods, 4, 14, 15
wheels, 10–11

XM30 rocket, 17